See It Grow

SUNFLOWER

by Joyce Markovics

Consultant: Karen C. Hall, PhD
Applied Ecologist, Botanical Research Institute of Texas
Fort Worth, Texas

BEARPORT
PUBLISHING

New York, New York

Credits

Title Page, © cooperr/Shutterstock; TOC, © Olaf Simon/iStock; 4–5, © Nadiia Korol/Shutterstock; 6–7, © Bogdan Wankowicz/Shutterstock; 6T, © Abel Tumik/Shutterstock; 6B, © AntiMartina/Shutterstock; 8L, © Ziva_K/iStock; 8R, © Kletr/Shutterstock; 9, © Shestakoff/Shutterstock; 10, © zcw/Shutterstock; 11, © bentaboe/iStock; 12–13, © Dr Ajay Kumar Singh/Shutterstock; 14, © Sergio33/Shutterstock; 15, © Piyaphon/Shutterstock; 16, © hkratky/iStock; 17, © Stana/iStock; 18, © PeterJSeager/iStock; 19, © stock_shot/Shutterstock; 20, © spfotocz/Shutterstock; 21, © Zvone/Shutterstock; 22, © Nataliia Melnychuk/Shutterstock; 23 (T to B), © Antonio D'Albore/iStock, © SumikoPhoto/iStock, © ifong/Shutterstock, © Kungverylucky/Shutterstock, and © jaxmaxsr/iStock.

Publisher: Kenn Goin
Senior Editor: Joyce Tavolacci
Creative Director: Spencer Brinker
Design: Debrah Kaiser
Photo Researcher: Olympia Shannon

Library of Congress Cataloging-in-Publication Data

Markovics, Joyce L., author.
 Sunflower / by Joyce Markovics.
    pages cm. — (See it grow)
 Includes bibliographical references and index.
 ISBN 978-1-62724-843-3 (library binding : alk. paper) — ISBN 1-62724-843-9 (library binding : alk. paper)
 1. Sunflowers—Juvenile literature. I. Title. II. Series: See it grow.
 QK495.C74M27 2016
 583'.99—dc23

                    2015007543

For more information, write to Bearport Publishing Company, Inc., 45 West 21st Street, Suite 3B, New York, New York 10010. Printed in the United States of America.

10 9 8 7 6 5 4 3 2 1

Contents

Sunflower

In summer, tall sunflowers grow in fields.

Each plant has a huge yellow flower.

How did it get that way?

Sunflowers can grow taller than people.

Every sunflower starts out as a seed.

After the seed is planted and watered, it grows.

seed

First, **roots** stretch into the moist soil.

Then a green **shoot** pokes out of the ground.

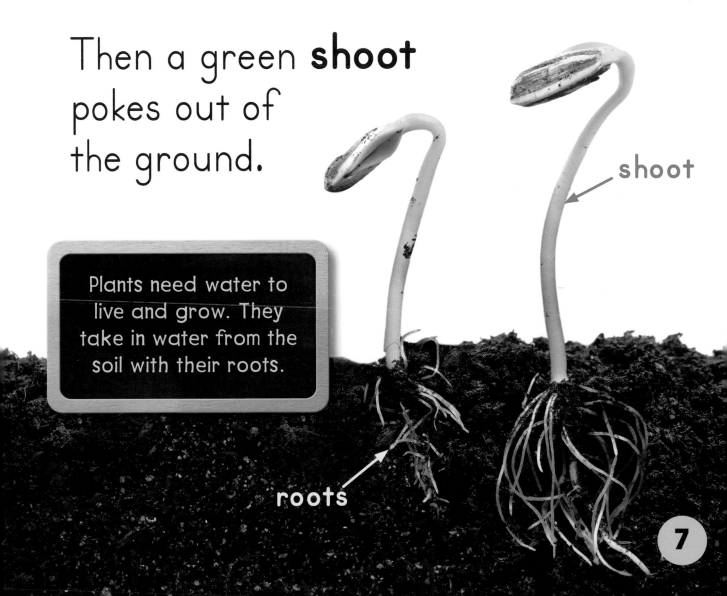

shoot

Plants need water to live and grow. They take in water from the soil with their roots.

roots

As the days pass, the tiny plant grows leaves.

Its **stem** gets taller and thicker.

stem

Leaves use the sun's light to make food for the plant.

9

At the top of the stem, a small **bud** forms.

During the day, the bud and leaves bend toward the sun.

bud

Sunflowers try to get as much light as possible. Sunlight helps them grow.

The bud gets bigger
and bigger.

Soon, the bud opens.

petals

Large yellow petals surround the center of the flower.

13

In the center of
the big flower are
many tiny flowers.

They are shaped
like tubes.

tiny
flower

The flowering part
of the sunflower is
called the head.

15

Bees fly to the tiny flower tubes.

16

There, they collect **pollen** to use for food.

As the bees fly from plant to plant, they spread the pollen.

Pollen helps make new plants.

After a while, the flower tubes get darker.

A black seed forms in each one.

Then the seeds dry out.

They fall to the ground.

Birds and chipmunks love to eat sunflower seeds.

Next year, some of the new seeds will grow.

They will become big, tall sunflowers!

People grow
sunflowers in gardens.
They also grow them
on large farms.

Sunflower Facts

- There are many kinds of sunflowers. Some are short and small, while others are big and tall.

- Sunflower seeds are eaten as snacks. They are also made into cooking oil.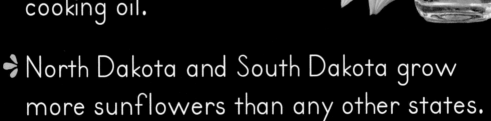

- North Dakota and South Dakota grow more sunflowers than any other states.

- The tallest sunflower in the world grew to be more than 26 feet (8 m) tall.

Glossary

 **bud** (BUHD) a small growth on the stem of a plant that turns into a leaf or flower

 **pollen** (POL-in) tiny yellow grains made by flowering plants; plants use pollen to help make new plants

 **roots** (ROOTS) parts of a plant that take in water and food from the soil

 **shoot** (SHOOT) a young plant that has just appeared above the soil

stem (STEM) the upright part of a plant that connects the roots to the leaves and flowers

23

Index

Read More

Bodach, Vijaya Khisty. *Flowers (Plant Parts).* North Mankato, MN: Capstone (2007).

Lawrence, Ellen. *Cooking with Sunshine: How Plants Make Food (Plant-ology).* New York: Bearport (2013).

Learn More Online

To learn more about sunflowers, visit
www.bearportpublishing.com/SeeItGrow

About the Author

Joyce Markovics lives in Tarrytown, New York.
She and her husband grow mammoth Russian sunflowers.